Haunted City

Joel T. Rose

published by Pure Cinema Press

"But only one is a wanderer.
Two together are always going somewhere."

—Alfred Hitchcock's *Vertigo*.

"What's under the underworld?" you ask.

I hesitate to answer:

Because I know we'll have to find out.

Because a question in a dream is an oath.

Because I know one of us will never come back.

I take a deep breath then answer:

"Meet me in the haunted city."

You'll know you're in the right place when the river glows brighter than the sky just after sunset.

And every flower is a lonely flower,
destroying your memories of all other flowers.

The cafes are empty and ordinary but evocative of your youth.
You feel like writing poetry there,
but one line disappears as soon as you write the next.

"I could never live here," you say,
"with all the cinemas empty and decaying and full of ghosts."

We wander into empty houses. I'm too afraid to go down the stairs when I hear the old songs they're singing below.

We pass so many lonely buildings with broken
windows, I lose count after a thousand.

In the middle of town we leave the streets and take to the alleys.
They're my favorite part of the haunted city. I feel safe here holding your
hand and walking slowly, listening to the cicadas.

What holy sites are these?
So many sacred spaces and eerie grottos …

We float over the tall fences separating the city from the forest.
When we come back an hour later the fences are gone.

We forget who we are, and the buildings do, too.

Ready to see ghosts, we enter places we shouldn't
and sing sacred songs in every holy place.

Ghosts are lonelier when they're trees.

Human forms are rare,
and usually we see them in destroyed houses …

... or from a distance and by water.

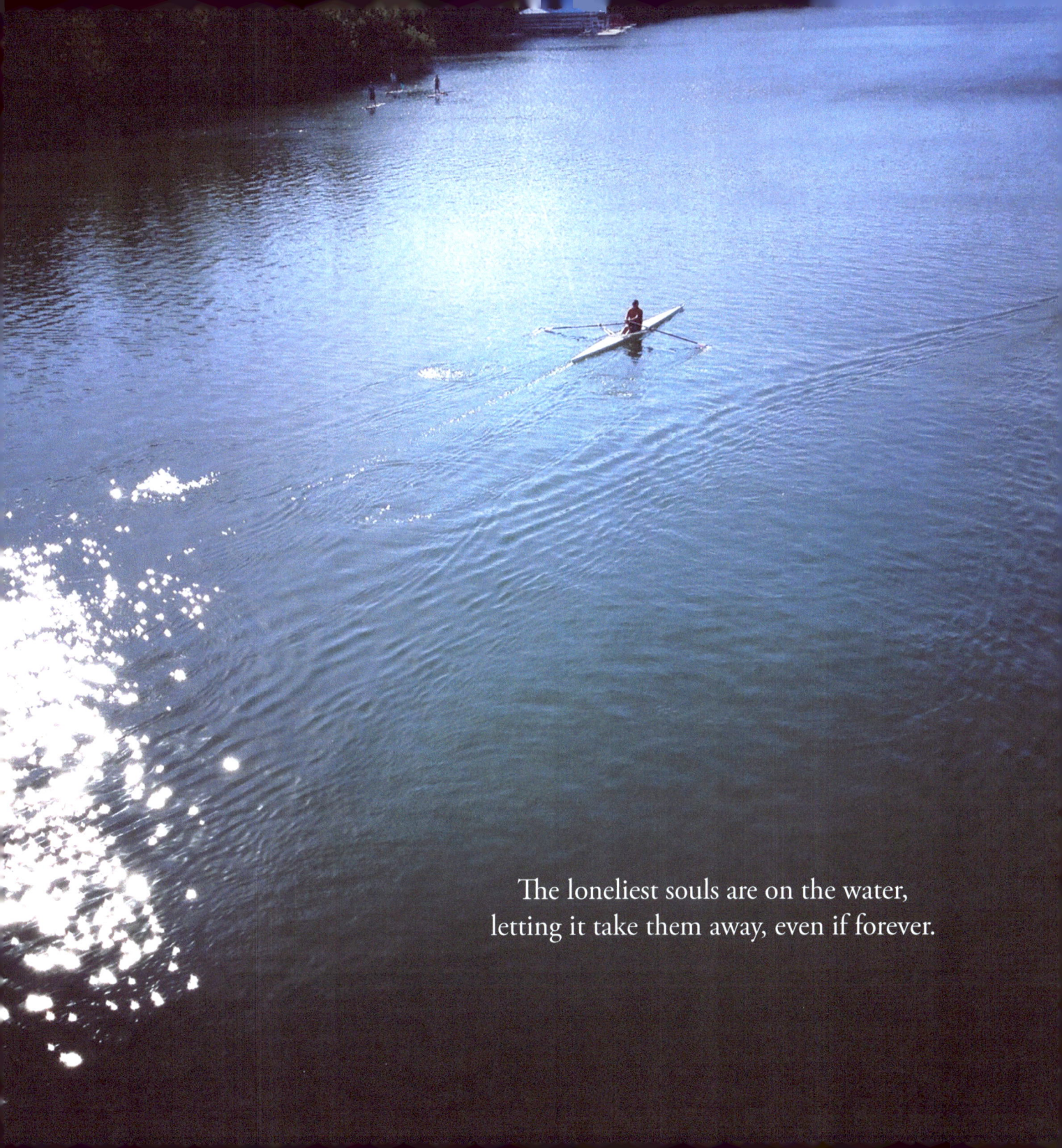

The loneliest souls are on the water,
letting it take them away, even if forever.

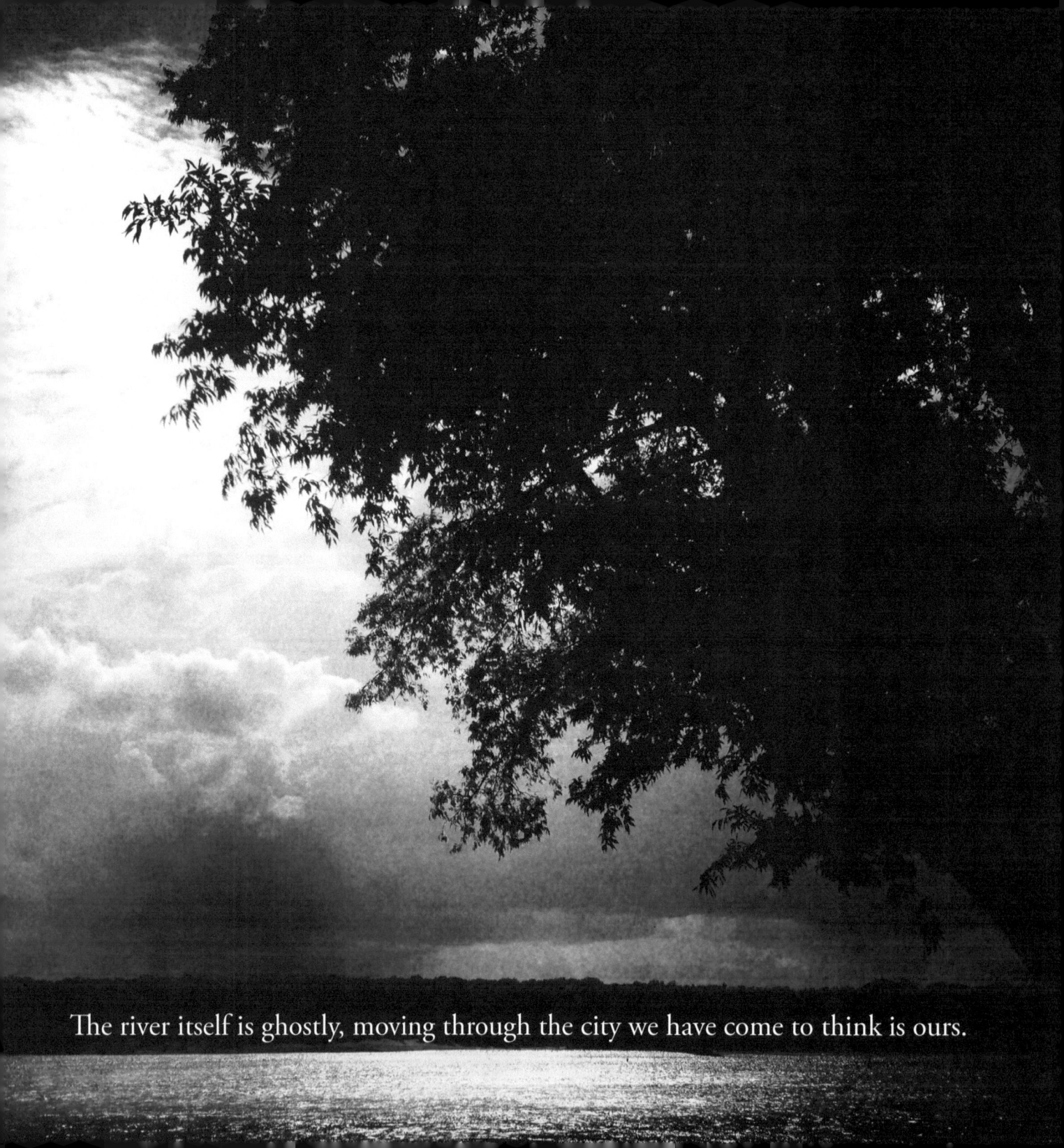

The river itself is ghostly, moving through the city we have come to think is ours.

We wander alone for a while,
promising to meet up again when
the holy places have fallen
and the profane rises again.

You forget me, and I you.
We've passed through too many doors and dreams
(and dreams which are doors).

People gathered here for some purpose,
for reasons lost as time obliterates all memories of
memories within this city.

Goodbye.

I feel like I knew a lover, had her here with me.
She would have loved this place.

I forget how much I've forgotten.

It's the air, these lonely trees.

Look at all these golfers and other sports enthusiasts.

I feel your presence, but I've forgotten your name.

I meet this cat. He tells me of a woman who scratched his chest and told him secrets. I ask him, "When?" and he says it was long before he became a cat.

I feel you watching me from somewhere.
When I see shattered things, your face floats in front of me for a moment,
then disappears back to the place the cat lived before he was a cat.

Objects here are all lonely. They whisper things whispered to them when you were here—which I'm starting to think was a long time ago indeed.

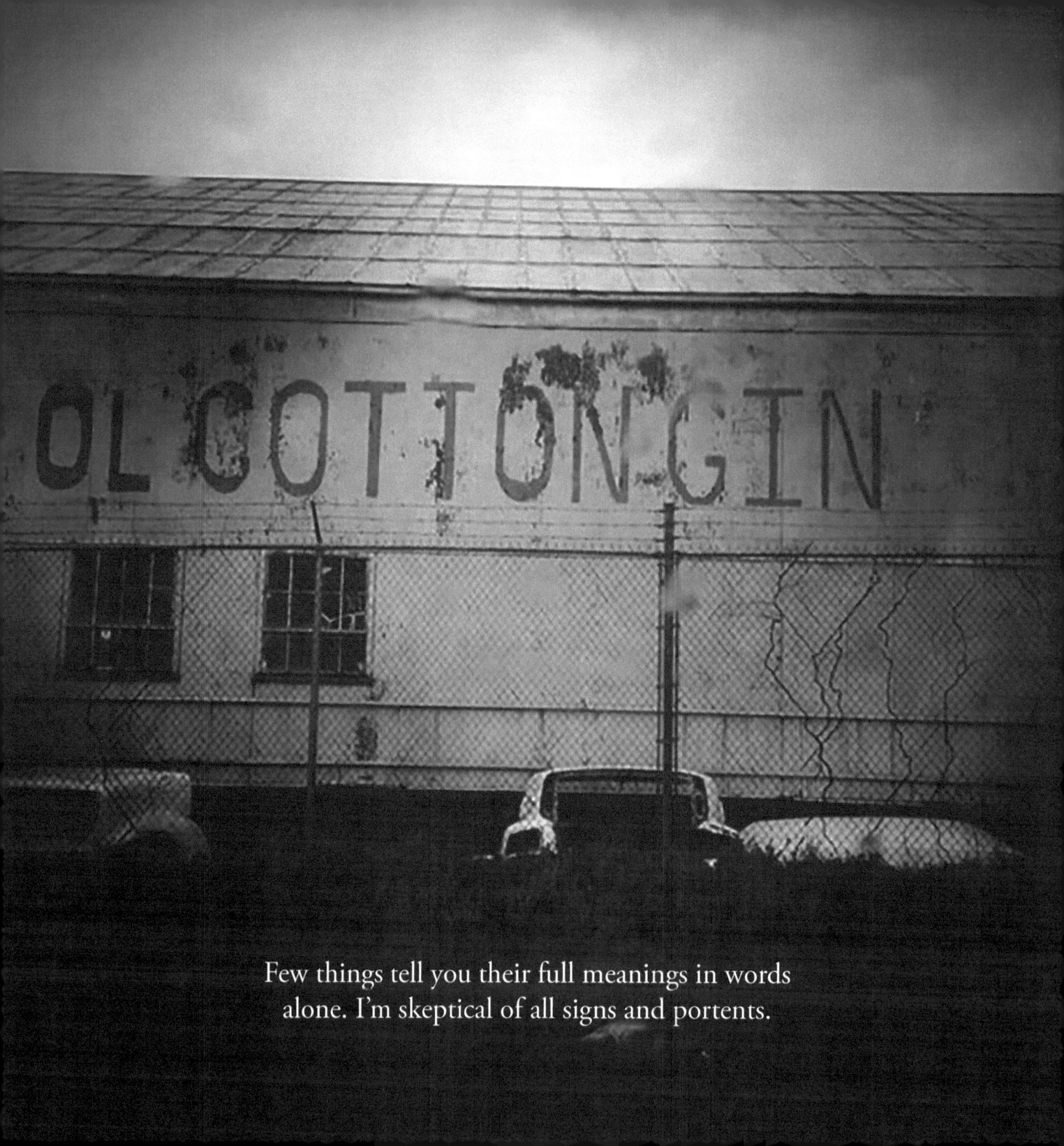

OL COTTON GIN

Few things tell you their full meanings in words
alone. I'm skeptical of all signs and portents.

Your voice in my head again: Remember to regret losing me.

You're really back by my side for a moment.
I listen to a hundred stories of your days and nights in the haunted city.
You say we arrived by train,
but I have an instinct you may be lying.

I show you the alleys I love so much,
and you laugh because you say you showed them to me long ago.

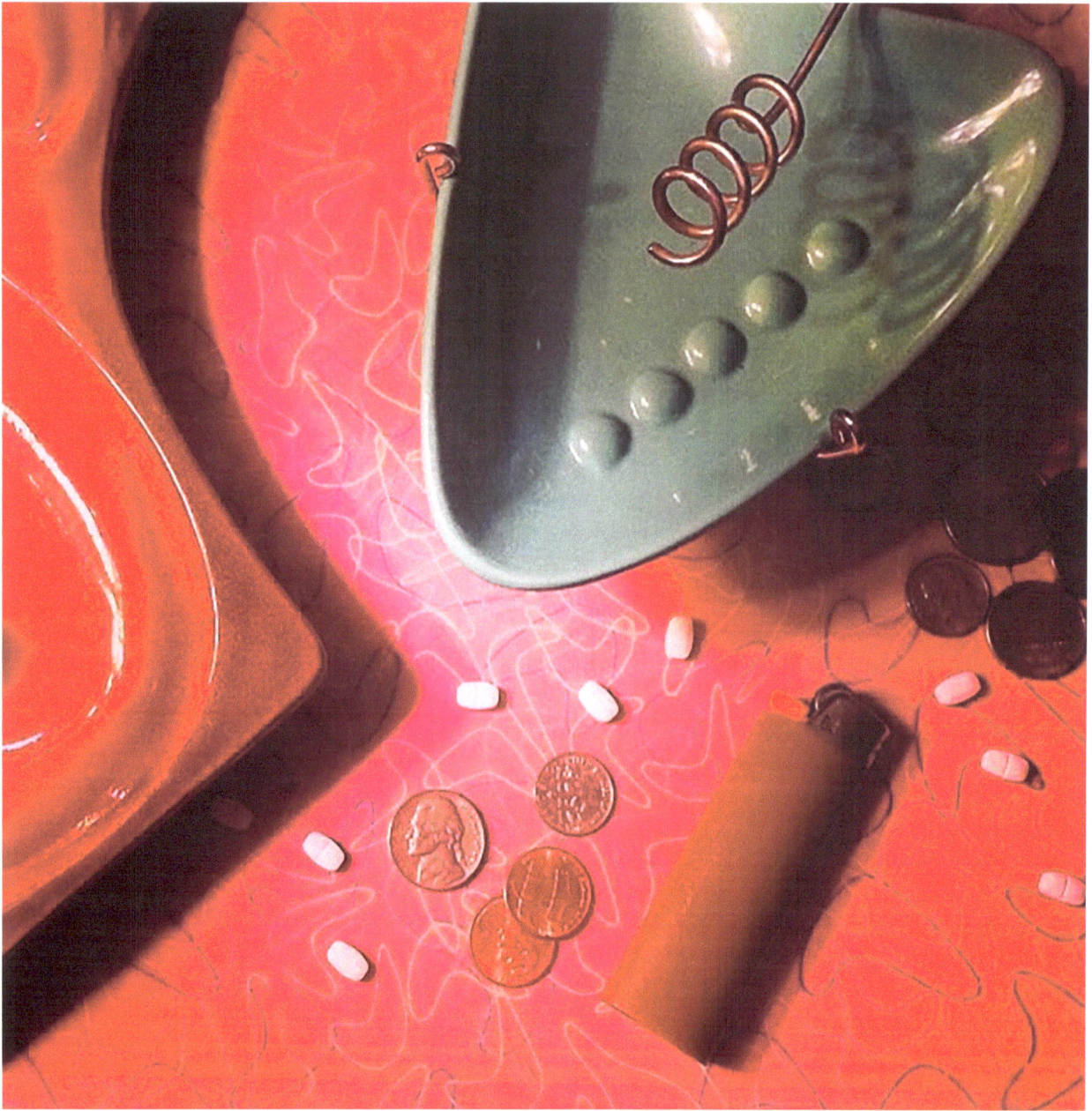

Finally we find a room in an abandoned house that seems freshly vacated—
like the ghosts were just here moments ago.

The river might be why this place is haunted.
Light doesn't behave here like it's supposed to.

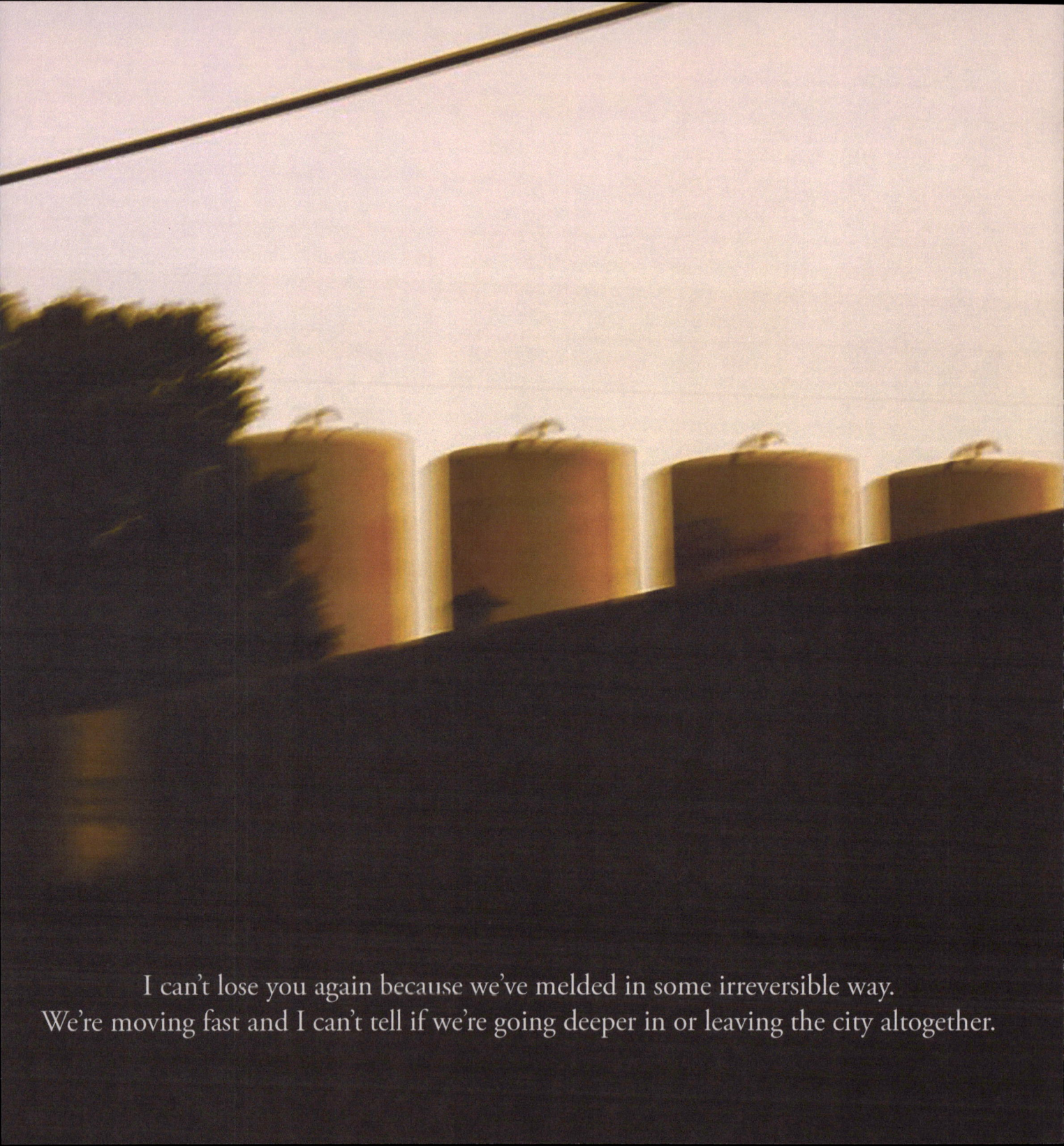

I can't lose you again because we've melded in some irreversible way.
We're moving fast and I can't tell if we're going deeper in or leaving the city altogether.

The city stops making sense, even in the surreal and ghostly ways it used to.

Somehow we know if we leave,
there is nothing under this underworld.

I'm this old road.

You are these clouds.

This moment reminds me of yesterday.

Everything reminds me of you. You put the fun in fungus.

Freight is also freighted. It's too quiet here.

The ruins everywhere make me wonder aloud,
"When weren't we here?"

I remember other cities,
but you say that there is only one.

Nothing more than this.

We are abstract, too.

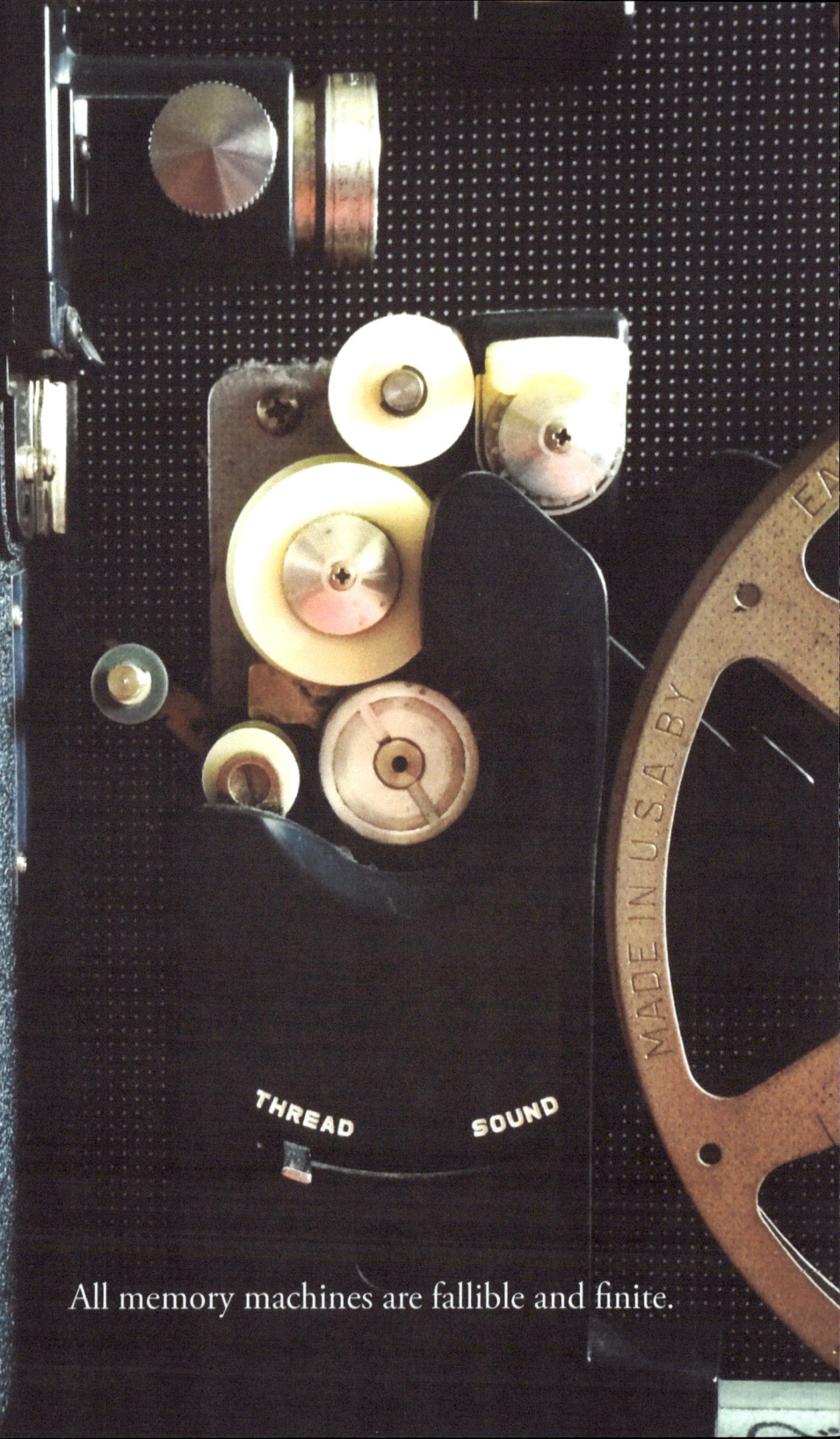

Kodak

STILL

24

REVERSE   FORWARD

16

Kodak

Sound 8
PROJECTOR   MODEL 1

ON

OFF   OFF

LAMP   LAMP
NORMAL   BRIGHT

THREAD   SOUND

MADE IN U.S.A. BY

All memory machines are fallible and finite.

All clouds glow with sorrow.

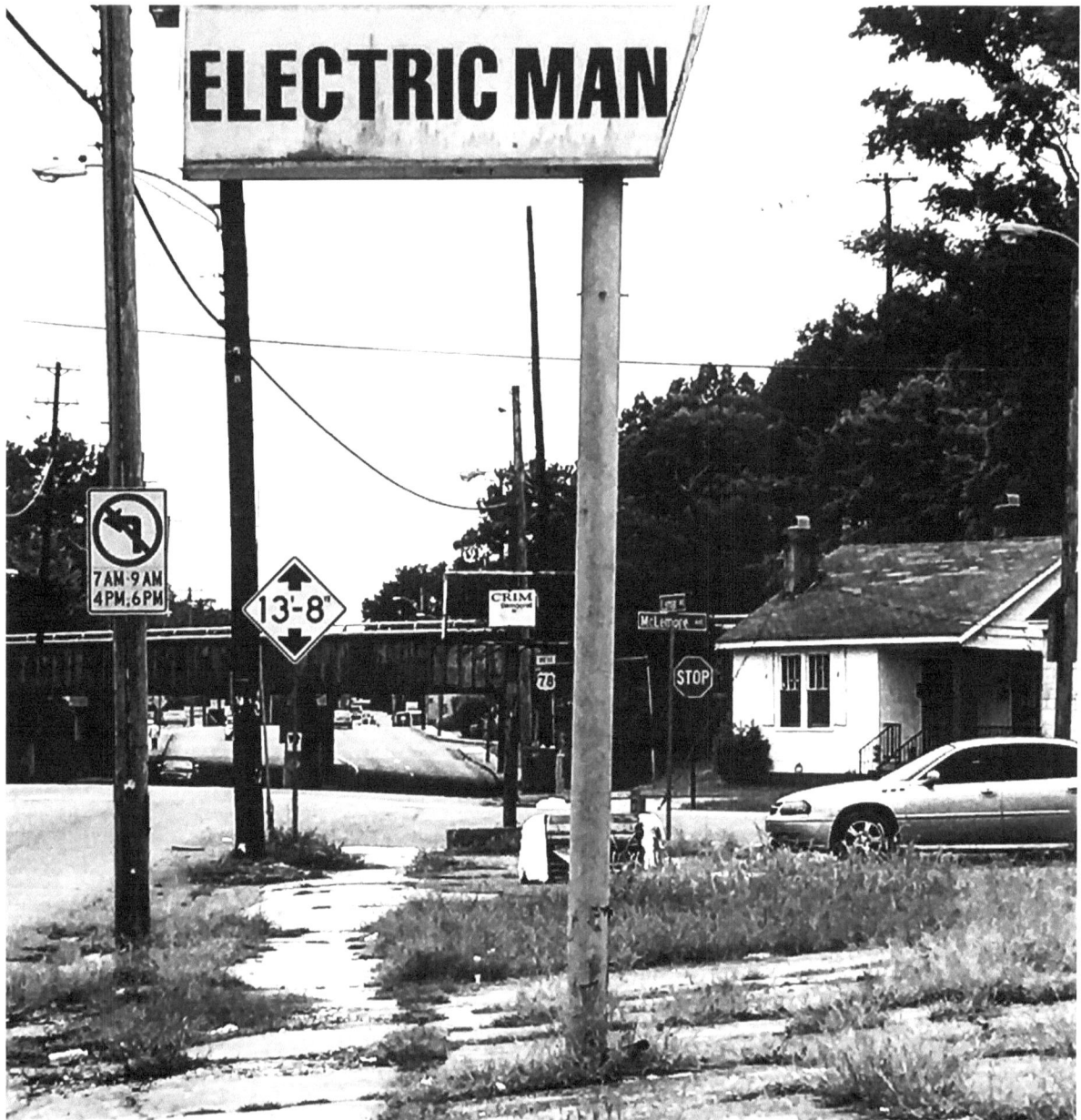

After this we'll sleep.

After this we'll memorize these buildings.

Inside these structures the lost souls are piled up like loose
dry sheets of paper from a thousand books.

And the cities bleed into one another again, until there is just one,
until they've bled out.

Was this palm in M———— or L—— ————?

Three words but not the ones you expected: Let's Get Lost.

Cities are definitely folding into one another now,
and the hybrids are the saddest and prettiest illusions of them all.

If the Blues make you forgetful
the Oranges obliterate memories before they can be forgotten.

But I'm tired and looking for another season.
When it's night, it's the season of empty
job sites and forgotten lovers.

If it's winter again,
I'll know you were never here with me.

I think Madeline was wrong.

Two can be wanderers and get lost together,
lost together but alone.

www.ingramcontent.com/pod-product-compliance
Lightning Source LLC
Chambersburg PA
CBHW040915100426
42737CB00042B/87